Contents

Warrior Elite

To conquer and maintain his huge empire, 8th-century Frankish king Charlemagne needed warriors that could travel and fight on horseback. In return for oaths of loyalty he gave them land – and the concept of the medieval knight was born.

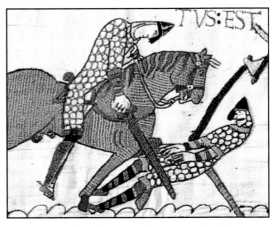

A Norman knight cuts down Anglo-Saxon King Harold II in 1066. The Norman conquest brought knights to England.

SERVICE

Knights were vassals (servants) to noblemen, called lords. The knights paid homage to their lords, pledging reverence and submission. The knight himself would rent the land awarded to him to villeins (peasants) and freemen, and some of these would repay him with military service. Some knights could call up small armies this way.

Knights also had servants called squires – usually the teenaged sons of nobles. Squires travelled with their knights and were trained in

how to become knights themselves. Ultimately all peasants, squires, knights, lords and barons were vassals to the king (who owned most of the land). He called on them when wars had to be fought.

CHIVALRY

A knight had to be gallant, loyal and had to swear against selfishness and cowardice – in short he had to be an excellent soldier. This code of chivalry extended to protecting defenceless widows, children and elders (but not peasants).

Soldiers could be knighted for brave deeds or before battle to give them courage.

Grap History

KNIGHTS

By Gary Jeffrey & Illustrated by Nick Spender

W
FRANKLIN WATTS
LONDON•SYDNEY

Franklin Watts
First published in Great Britain in 2018 by
The Watts Publishing Group

Designed by Gary Jeffrey and illustrated by Nick Spender

HB ISBN 978 1 4451 6687 2
PB ISBN 978 1 4451 6688 9

Printed in Malaysia

Franklin Watts
An imprint of
Hachette Children's Group
Part of The Watts Publishing Group
Carmelite House
50 Victoria Embankment
London EC4Y 0DZ

An Hachette UK Company
www.hachette.co.uk

www.franklinwatts.co.uk

GRAPHIC MEDIEVAL HISTORY KNIGHTS
was produced for Franklin Watts by
David West Children's Books, 11 Glebe Road, London SW13 0DR

Photo credits:
p5 middle, Anagoria

EQUIPPING A KNIGHT

A knight's most valuable piece of equipment was his warhorse – a highly trained animal known as a destrier. He also needed a packhorse and a palfrey for his travels. Before the 14th century his main weapon was a sharp, doubled-edged sword. Until plate armour was invented (see page 6) long-sleeved chainmail shirts (hauberks) and leggings were used for armour. A large shield displayed the knight's coat of arms.

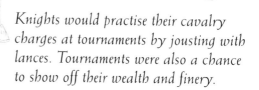

Knights would practise their cavalry charges at tournaments by jousting with lances. Tournaments were also a chance to show off their wealth and finery.

The great helm, or bucket helm, was popular with knights in the 13th century. It gave great protection but had no air holes and was hard to see out of. Eventually it was used only as a jousting helm.

CRUSADING KNIGHTS

In 1095 Pope Urban II called for the Holy Land to be reclaimed from Muslims for Christian pilgrimage. Over the next 200 years many knights 'took up the cross' on the understanding that, in return for military service on crusades, they would be forgiven for all of their sins.

These early 14th-century battling knights wear great helms and surcoats over their mail. They wield sharp, pointed swords that were very effective in piercing the rings of mail armour.

Knights in Battle

During the 14th century pieces of plate armour, moulded to fit the body, began to appear on the shoulders, chests and legs of knights. Specialist armourers appeared in Italy and Germany. By 1400 the rich, fashionable knight was dressed from head to toe in metal.

A 15th-century artwork of the Battle of Crécy (1346) when English archers first defeated French knights.

A HUNDRED YEARS WAR

A succession crisis in France in 1328 caused England's King Edward III to declare himself king of France. In 1346 he invaded France, won a great victory at Crécy and also captured Calais, which became an English garrison.

In 1356 his son, Edward, the 'Black Prince', invaded and won another great victory at Poitiers. France fell into chaos and Edward III invaded again, intending to be crowned at Reims. However the town resisted his siege and all his gains, except for Calais, were lost.

The 14th-century bascinet evolved from the steel cap worn under a great helm. A mail 'aventail' collar protected the throat. The best helms also had snout-like visors.

Forty-five years later, recently-crowned Henry V saw his chance and invaded while France was ravaged by civil war. After a struggle taking the port of Harfleur Henry headed his troops towards Calais…

By 1429 England's conquest of France had reached its greatest extent. But at the Siege of Orléans (left) a visionary peasant girl called Joan (below), backed and equipped by knights, had an extraordinary effect.

WARS OF THE ROSES

Edward III created the first English dukedoms and awarded them to his sons, making them hugely powerful. The death of his eldest son, Edward, the Black Prince, a year before his father in 1376 sparked an epic feud between the descendants (and their supporters) of the younger sons over who had the right to rule.

Club-like weapons like the mace were effective at breaking through the new plate armour.

The two most powerful lines were the House of York (the white rose) and the House of Lancaster (a red rose). In 1399 the Black Prince's son, Richard II, was deposed by his brother's son, Henry IV (Lancaster). The Lancasters ruled until Henry VI was deposed by Edward IV, the first Yorkist king, who practically wiped out the Lancastrian line at the Battle of Towton in 1461. The only challenger left was the Lancastrian heir, Henry Tudor.

By the time of the climax of the Wars of the Roses at Bosworth (see page 32) the top knights were wearing full gothic-style plate armour. The distinctive slitted helmet was called a sallet. A metal chin-piece (a bevor) protected the neck. The armour was articulated (moved at the joints) and weighed about the same as modern army kits.

The Battle of Agincourt

OCTOBER 25TH 1415, THE OPEN LAND BETWEEN THE WOODS OF TRAMECOURT AND AGINCOURT IN NORTHERN FRANCE.

PREPARE TO ADVANCE.

AGAINST THE USUAL MILITARY STRATEGY OF THE TIME ENGLISH KING HENRY V WAS MAKING THE FIRST MOVE AGAINST THE FRENCH ARMY SPREAD BEFORE HIM.

AS THE COMMAND PASSED THROUGH THE RANKS EACH MAN FELL TO HIS KNEES, KISSED THE GROUND AND PUT A SMALL PIECE OF EARTH IN HIS MOUTH.

MANY OF THE 9,000 MEN WERE SICK WITH DYSENTERY AND ALL WERE TIRED AND HUNGRY.

AGAINST THEM STOOD AT LEAST 12,000 - THE CREAM OF FRENCH ARMS, BARRING THE ROUTE TO THE ENGLISH FORTRESS AT CALAIS, AND REFUGE.

THE KNIGHTS STRUGGLED THROUGH THE HEAVY CLAY.

IN THE VANGUARD THE MEN TRUDGED THROUGH THE RAIN-SOAKED GROUND, MADE WORSE BY THE CHURNING OF HUNDREDS OF HORSES' HOOVES.

THE ENGLISH ARCHERS HELD THEIR BOWS READY, AND WAITED...

...FOR THE SIGNAL...

NOW, STRIKE!

ALL 7,000 RAISED THEIR BOWS AND FIRED.

IN AN INSTANT THE SKY WAS DARK WITH ARROWS...

THUK!

THUK!

THUK!

AAAGH!

...FALLING LIKE DEADLY RAIN.

14

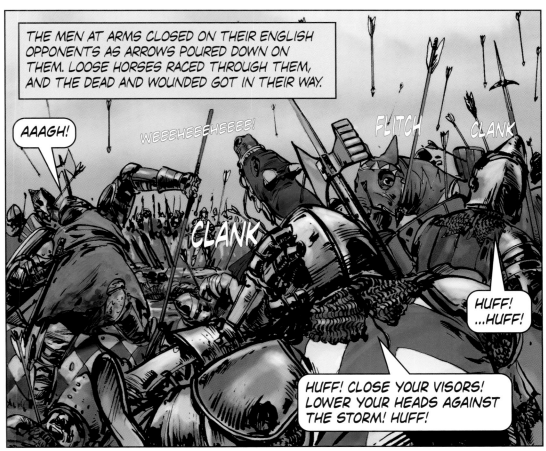

THE FRENCH FORWARD LINE CRASHED INTO THE ENGLISH AND WAS MOMENTARILY THROWN BACK BEFORE THEY SURGED AGAIN. THE COMBAT WAS VICIOUSLY HAND-TO-HAND.

THE BOWMEN LEVELLED THEIR AIM AND FIRED POINT BLANK INTO THE CROWDS OF FRENCH KNIGHTS.

RAPIDLY THEY PICKED OFF TARGETS.

FWUFFF...

THUNK

AAAAAGH!

RAAAAAAAAAAGH!

NO ARROWS LEFT, THEY DROPPED THEIR BOWS AND PITCHED IN WITH SWORDS, HATCHETS AND MALLETS.

RAAAAAAAAAAAGH!

CLANGGG

THEY FOUGHT WITH BLIND FURY, KNOWING THAT NONE OF THEM WOULD BE SPARED AS PRISONERS IF THEY LOST THE BATTLE.

THE WORN OUT, SLOW-MOVING FRENCH KNIGHTS WERE AT THE MERCY OF THE ENGLISH MEN AT ARMS.

FIGHTING IN THE CENTRE HENRY'S BROTHER, THE DUKE OF GLOUCESTER, SUDDENLY FELL FROM A VIOLENT THRUST.

ARRRGH!

SKINK

WORD QUICKLY REACHED THE KING.

HUMPHREY!?

MEN! COME WITH ME!

WAVE UPON WAVE OF FRENCH KNIGHTS SURGED FORWARDS, HEEDLESS OF THOSE IN FRONT, EAGER TO GET AT HENRY AND AVENGE THE TAKING OF HARFLEUR.

KRINK

WOOARGH!

NYAAAARGH!

SKUNCH

GUUURGLE...

THE PILE OF FALLEN IN FRONT OF THE KING'S STANDARD (FLAG) GREW ENORMOUS. AS THE LIVING FELL ALONGSIDE THE DEAD, MANY SUFFOCATED UNDER THE WEIGHT, OR WERE FORCED DOWN INTO THE MUD AND DROWNED.

The Siege of Orléans

MAY 7TH 1429, A FRENCH EFFORT TO BREAK THE SIEGE OF ORLÉANS IN NORTH CENTRAL FRANCE WAS NOT GOING WELL. THEY HAD BEEN INSPIRED BY FRENCH MAID, JOAN OF ARC, TO ATTACK THE ENGLISH-HELD FORT, THE TOURELLES, AT THE SOUTH END OF ORLÉANS BRIDGE.

THAK!

AAAAAGHHH

ATTEMPTS TO UNDERMINE THE FOUNDATIONS AND SET FIRE TO THE FORT'S BASTION HAD FAILED. IF THE ENGLISH WERE REINFORCED AND THE CITY FELL THE REST OF FRANCE COULD BE LOST.

NOW A DESPERATE EFFORT WAS BEING MADE TO SCALE THE BASTION'S WALLS, WITH JOAN OF ARC HERSELF IN THE BREACH.

COME ON! LET'S GET THIS LADDER *UP!*

DIRECTLY ABOVE, A CROSSBOWMAN TOOK AIM.

RIGHT! YOU WITCH...

'...I HAVE YOU NOW!'

WHILE DUNOIS CALLED BACK THE MEN, JOAN WENT INTO A NEARBY VINEYARD FOR A QUIET MOMENT OF PRAYER.

COME ON - THE MAID SAYS WE HAVE TO RALLY.

SUDDENLY BURSTING FROM THE TREES JOAN SEIZED HER STANDARD AND GALLOPED TOWARDS THE FORT.

DURRUM-DURRUM-DURRUM-DURRUM

JAMMING THE STANDARD IN THE DITCH AT THE BASE OF THE WALL SHE SHOUTED WITH ALL HER MIGHT...

CHAAARGE!

AS THE MEN SWARMED UP THE LADDERS JOAN TURNED TO HER PAGE, DE CONTES.

RAAAAAA!

WHEN THE WIND CARRIES THE BANNER TO THE WALL, *IT WILL BE OURS!*

SWISSSHHH

SMOKE WAS MYSTERIOUSLY BILLOWING FROM THE RIVER SIDE OF THE BASTION.

EVERYONE, BACK TO THE KEEP!

THE WITCH - SHE'S ALIVE!

JOAN CAME FORWARD AND ADDRESSED THE BACK OF THE GARRISON'S COMMANDER...

GLASDALE, SURRENDER TO THE KING OF HEAVEN!

GLASDALE AND HIS KNIGHTS THUNDERED ACROSS THE BURNING DRAWBRIDGE TOWARDS THE KEEP ON THE RIVER.

OUT OF THE WAY!

THE BRIDGE SUDDENLY GAVE WAY, PLUNGING THE KNIGHTS INTO THE FIRE BARGE THAT BURNED BELOW.

AIEEEEEEEEEEEE!

MEANWHILE, ON THE OTHER SIDE OF THE TOURELLES, SOME OF THE FRENCH MILITIA LOWERED A ROUGH FOOTBRIDGE ACROSS THE BROKEN SPAN OF ORLÉANS BRIDGE.

ALLEZ! ALLEZ!

WITH THEIR CROSSING DISGUISED BY DARKNESS AND SMOKE, THE MILITIA SEEMED TO COME FROM NOWHERE TO SEIZE THE KEEP.

DROP IT!

THE NEXT DAY THE ENGLISH CAME OUT OF THE FORTS SURROUNDING ORLÉANS AND TOOK UP POSITIONS AS IF TO FIGHT, BUT THEN TURNED AND MARCHED AWAY.

WATCHING THEM LEAVE, JOAN WAS BOTH ELATED AND RELIEVED.

YES! THEY ARE RETREATING. LET THEM GO WHILE WE GIVE THANKS TO GOD!

THE RAPID AND UNEXPECTED VICTORY OVER THE BESIEGERS WAS THE SIGN JOAN HAD PROMISED THE DAUPHIN* AT POITIERS TWO MONTHS BEFORE. NOW HER MISSION WAS TO SEE HIM CROWNED KING OF FRANCE.

THE END

* FRENCH HEIR TO THE THRONE

The Battle of Bosworth

ON 22ND AUGUST 1485, AT AMBION HILL, NEAR BOSWORTH IN THE HEART OF ENGLAND, A BATTLE WAS RAGING.

KING RICHARD III WAS AN EXPERIENCED SOLDIER AND, AS EVER, IT WAS HARD TO SEE EXACTLY WHO WAS WINNING IN THE CHAOS LAID OUT BEFORE HIM, WHEN SUDDENLY...

...THERE HE IS!

HE HAD CAUGHT SIGHT OF HENRY TUDOR, THE MAN WHO WAS CHALLENGING HIM FOR THE THRONE OF ENGLAND.

CRUNCH

THEY WERE QUICKLY SPOTTED.

TUDOR! GET DOWN OFF YOUR HORSE. WE WILL PROTECT YOU.

HENRY WAS NO WAR LEADER.

PIKEMEN AT THE REAR OF HIS VANGUARD WERE ORDERED BACK AT THE RUN...

FORM A SQUARE. PROTECT THE PRINCE!

...AND QUICKLY ARRANGED INTO A FORMATION BRISTLING WITH SPEARS.

UNLIKE RICHARD, TUDOR HAD BEEN FORCED TO HIRE A ROUGH BAND OF MERCENARIES, AND PIKEMEN 'BORROWED' FROM FRANCE.

RICHARD'S DIVISON CAME THUNDERING IN AND INSTANTLY MET AN UNWAVERING WALL OF SPIKES.

HORSES WERE SPEARED AND MEN FELL LEFT AND RIGHT...

...INCLUDING THE KING...

CURSE YOU!

THE FAILED CHARGE HAD BEEN WATCHED BY SIR WILLIAM STANLEY. HE HAD STOOD BY WITH HIS FORCE TO SEE WHETHER TUDOR'S MEN WOULD WIN.

NOW HE WAS SURE...

DEATH TO RICHARD - THE USURPER!

FOLLOWING HIS BROTHER, KING EDWARD IV'S DEATH, RICHARD III HAD BECOME ROYAL PROTECTOR TO EDWARD'S YOUNG SON, UNTIL HE CAME OF AGE.

YOUNG PRINCE EDWARD AND HIS BROTHER, THE DUKE OF YORK, HAD BEEN TAKEN TO THE TOWER OF LONDON. GRADUALLY THEY WERE SEEN LESS AND LESS OFTEN, UNTIL THEY WERE SEEN NO MORE...

MEANWHILE, TO PREVENT EDWARD'S IN-LAWS FROM GAINING THE THRONE, RICHARD HAD MADE HIMSELF KING.

WHILE MANY PEOPLE WERE HAPPY FOR HIM TO BE KING, THERE WAS A SUSPICION THAT HE HAD MURDERED THE 'PRINCES IN THE TOWER' TO TAKE THEIR THRONE, AND THAT RUMOUR PERSISTED.

THE DOWNED KING WAS HELPED TO HIS FEET.

SIRE, WE'LL GET A HORSE AND TAKE YOU TO SAFETY!

A HORSE?

MY KINGDOM FOR A HORSE?

NO! WE WILL FINISH THIS!

KILLING TUDOR WOULD SECURE HIS RULE ONCE AND FOR ALL.

39

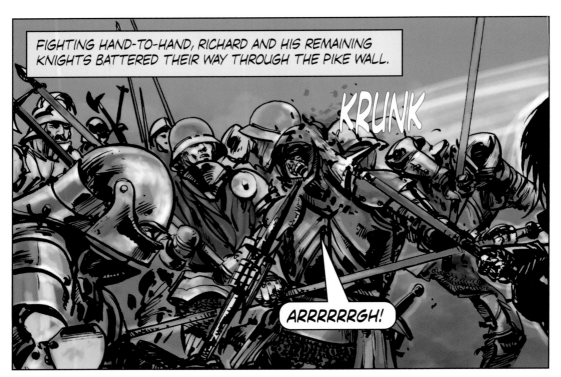

FIGHTING HAND-TO-HAND, RICHARD AND HIS REMAINING KNIGHTS BATTERED THEIR WAY THROUGH THE PIKE WALL.

KRUNK

ARRRRRRGH!

FINALLY, RICHARD REACHED TUDOR'S STANDARD BEARER...

NO! NO! BACK OFF!

...AND CHOPPED HIM DOWN.

THAK!

THE SHOCK IMPACT OF STANLEY'S FRESH TROOPS WAS TOO MUCH. SUDDENLY THE KING'S STANDARD BEARER WAS KNOCKED DOWN, SWIFTLY FOLLOWED BY THE KING HIMSELF.

UNHELMED AS HE WAS, RICHARD WAS HELPLESS TO RESIST THE FATAL, STABBING BLOW...

The End of Knights

Joan of Arc had risen from being a village elder's daughter to the 'knight' who inspired the last defence of France against the English invaders. After Orléans Joan went to the dauphin and convinced him to travel to Reims to be crowned.

DOWNFALL

Joan fought alongside French knights, conquering English forts that barred the route. At the village of Patay the English prepared an ambush, with archers surrounding their defences. But French scouts reported their positions to the

A 19th-century painting of Joan of Arc at the coronation of Charles VII.

knights. The French attacked and caught the longbowmen by surprise, slaughtering thousands of them – their revenge at last for Agincourt.

King Charles VII (Charles the Victorious), was crowned on 17th July 1429. Joan wanted to continue forcing the English from France but on 23rd May 1430 she was captured by Burgundians.

The Burgundians, who were allies of the English, had been besieging Compiègne. Joan was ransomed to the enemy for 10,000 gold crowns. She was put on trial for heresy, found guilty and burned at the stake in Rouen, on 30th May 1431. Four hundred and eighty-nine years later she was canonised as a saint.

NEW DYNASTY

Henry Tudor's claim to the throne was through his mother, Lady Margaret Beaufort, a great-granddaughter of John of Gaunt (Edward III's third surviving son). To strengthen his claim Henry married Richard III's daughter, Elizabeth of York. The marriage joined together the houses of Lancaster and York. He was crowned Henry VII on 23rd October 1485 and reigned for 24 years.

Henry VII was not a military man. He was a good administrator and kept control of the powerful nobles. He built up the navy and began the future Tudor dynasty.

Henry VII holds the Tudor rose, which is the roses of Lancaster and York combined. The Renaissance began with the Tudors.

HONORARY KNIGHTS

In the 15th century crude firearms were used for the first time. As these weapons developed full plate armour became increasingly impractical and ineffective.

Chivalric knighthoods are still awarded in the United Kingdom as honorary titles. The highest is the Most Noble Order of the Garter, which was first awarded by Edward III in 1348.

Sometimes called the 'last knight', Holy Roman Emperor Maximillian I (1486–1519) was famous for the splendid decoration of his armour.

45

Glossary

bascinet A small, light, pointed metal helmet with a visor.

bastion A projecting part of a fortification, designed to give soldiers some protection while allowing them to fire.

breach A gap in the fortifications or line of defence of an enemy, created by the bombardment of attacking forces.

canonised Declared by the Church to be a saint.

cavalry Soldiers who fight on horseback.

coat of arms The heraldic badge of a noble family, displayed on their shields and clothing in battle.

dauphin The title given to the heir to the throne of France.

deposed Overthrown and removed from a position of power.

dysentery A serious disease that causes diarrhoea and loss of blood.

freeman A rent-paying tenant who owed little or no service to the local lord.

gallant Chivalrous, courteous, respectful and polite.

garrison The group of soldiers stationed in a fort or town in order to defend it.

heresy An opinion or belief that goes against the accepted religion of the time.

Edward III gives his son, the 'Black Prince', part of France.

keep The innermost and strongest part or central tower of a medieval castle.

palfrey A light, docile, saddle horse.

pilgrimage A long journey to a sacred place or shrine.

Plantagenet A royal dynasty that provided 14 kings of England during the Middle Ages.

red rose The House of Lancaster's badge during the Wars of the Roses.

Renaissance The revival of classical art, architecture, literature and learning that originated in Italy in the 14th century and later spread throughout Europe, marking the transition from medieval to modern times.

scouts Soldiers who explore ahead of the main force to discover information about an opposing army's position, numbers and plans.

standard bearer A soldier who carries the standard (the banner or flag) of his army into battle.

vanguard The front, or first, troops to engage in a battle.

villeins Medieval peasants who worked their lord's land and paid him certain dues, or had obligations to him, in return for the use of it.

white rose The House of York's badge during the Wars of the Roses.

Yorkists massacre fleeing Lancastrians at the Battle of Towton.

Index